Introduction

This book supports students preparing for the OCR GCSE exam. The
book are carefully modelled after past papers and specifications of e
that the papers as a whole provide a rich and varied practice to mee   ...s of
GCSE mathematics with an appropriate difficulty.

Papers are designed to teach students the most easily applicable, reusable and fastest
solutions to typical problems, and utilise problems which target areas of maths which
students typically forget under the pressure of an exam. Solutions provided have been
reviewed by many students to ensure that they are easily understandable while being the
fastest and most re-applicable.

The practice papers cover the following six distinct topic areas:
1. Fundamental Number Operations
2. Algebra
3. Ratio, proportion, and rates of change
4. Geometry and measures
5. Probability
6. Statistics

After completing these practice papers, you should be able to:
1. Quickly formulate optimal solutions to any GCSE mathematics question.
2. More readily apply previously learnt skills on a question to question basis.

GCSE Mathematics Practice Papers comprises of 2 books, calculator and non-calculator.
Each book contains 4 full practice papers. For the book with calculator, each practice paper
contains 22 questions and solutions. The non-calculator book contains 20 questions and
solutions per paper.

Contents

Paper 1 (Non-Calculator)

Materials

For this paper you must have:
- mathematical instruments

You **must** not use a calculator

Time allowed

1 hour 30 minutes.

Instructions

- Use black ink. Draw diagrams in HB pencil.
- Answer all questions.
- You must answer the questions in the space provided. Do not write outside the box around each page or on blank pages.
- Do all rough work in this book. Cross through any work that you do not want to be marked.
- In all calculations, show clearly how you work out your answer.

Information

- The marks for questions are shown in brackets.
- The maximum mark is 100.

Advice

- Read each question carefully before you start to answer it.
- Keep an eye on the time.
- Try to answer every question.
- Check your answers if you have time at the end.

1(a)   Work out $(2+\sqrt{3})(2-\sqrt{3})$

....

....

....

         Answer…………………………   (3 marks)

1(b)   Without using a calculator, work out $\dfrac{\sqrt{32}+\sqrt{50}}{\sqrt{18}}$

        Show all your working.

....

....

....

         Answer…………………………   (3 marks)

2   By writing each number correct to 1 significant figure, find an approximate value

        for $\dfrac{\sqrt{9.115}\times10^{5}}{5.997\times10^{-4}}$

        Give your answer in standard form.

....

....

....

         Answer…………………………   (3 marks)

3   Average speed $=\dfrac{\text{distance}}{\text{time}}$

        If the distance is doubled and the time is halved, what happens to the average speed?

        Circle your answer.

        ×2   ×4   no change   ÷2   ÷4

....

....

                                                                (3 marks)

4 Jack received 25% more emails in December than in November. Jack received 250 emails in December. How many more emails did Jack receive in December than in November?

………………………………………………………………………..............

………………………………………………………………………..............

………………………………………………………………………..............

  Answer………………………………. (3 marks)

5 A plant is 6 cm high and growing at a steady rate of 0.2 cm every day.

5(a) After how many days will the height reach 11 cm?

………………………………………………………………………..............

………………………………………………………………………..............

………………………………………………………………………..............

  Answer………………………………. (3 marks)

5(b) If the plant is growing at a slower rate, what effect will this have on your answer to part (a)?

………………………………………………………………………..............

  Answer………………………………. (3 marks)

6 Jack is making some small snacks for a party. He cuts 1.2 kg of cheese into a number of 15g pieces. How many pieces does he have?

Jack says

I can cut it into 80 pieces.

Is he correct? Show how you decide.

………………………………………………………………………..............

………………………………………………………………………..............

………………………………………………………………………..............

  Answer………………………………. (3 marks)

12

3

7   Rearrange $\dfrac{1}{x} + \dfrac{1}{y} = \dfrac{1}{w}$ to make y the subject.

…………………………………………………………………………..........…

…………………………………………………………………………….........…

……………………………………………………………………………..........…

    Answer………………………………   (3 marks)

8   The price of a television is reduced by 30% for a sale.

    Afterwards, the sale price is increased by 40%.

    Jack says the television is now 10% more expensive than before the sale.

    Explain Jack's error and work out the correct percentage change in the price of the

    television from before the sale to after the sale.

…………………………………………………………………………….........…

……………………………………………………………………………..........…

……………………………………………………………………………..........…

    Answer………………………………   (3 marks)

9   The first four terms of a sequence are

    2   8   32   128

9(a)   Work out the next term.

…………………………………………………………………………….........…

……………………………………………………………………………..........…

……………………………………………………………………………..........…

    Answer………………………………   (3 marks)

9(b)   Find the nth term.

…………………………………………………………………………….........…

……………………………………………………………………………..........…

……………………………………………………………………………..........…

    Answer………………………………   (3 marks)

10   There are 9 counters in a bag.

There is a number on each counter.

$$\left(1\right)\left(1\right)\left(2\right)\left(2\right)\left(2\right)\left(3\right)\left(3\right)\left(3\right)\left(3\right)$$

Jack takes at random 2 counters from the bag.

He adds together the numbers on the 2 counters to get his Total.

10(a)   Complete and fully label the probability tree diagram to show the possible outcome.

First counter   Second counter

$\frac{2}{9}$ 1

                         2

                         3

....

....

(4 marks)

10(b)   Work out the probability that his Total is greater than 3.

Give your answer as a fraction in its simplest form.

....

....

....

Answer…………………………   (2 marks)

6

5

11   The table shows information about the number of fish caught by 29 people in a club in one day.

Jack is one of the 29 people in the club.

Number of fish	Frequency
0	2
1	6
2	10
3	8
5	2
8	1

The number of fish caught by him was the same as the median number of fish caught for his club.

Work out the number of fish caught by him.

....

....

....

Answer……………………………….   (3 marks)

12   The diagram below is made from three squares.

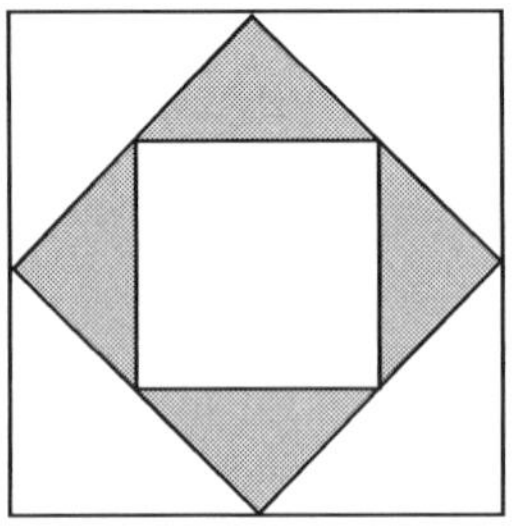

Find the ratio

 total shaded area : total unshaded area.

Give your answer in the simplest form.

....

....

....

Answer……………………………….   (3 marks)

13   Points A, B, C and D are on the circumference of a circle. AE is a tangent to the circle.

Work out ∠ACD

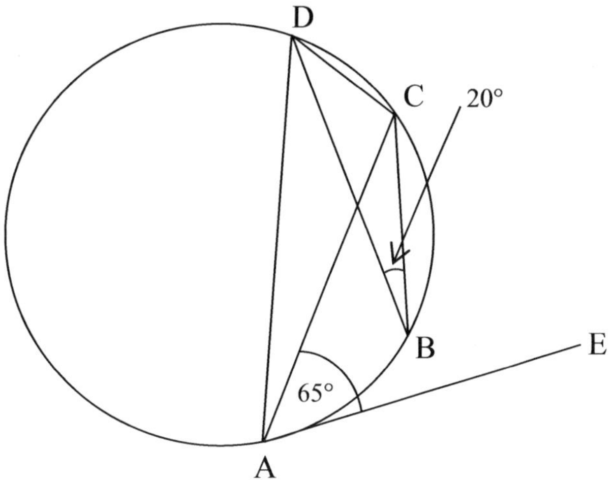

………………………………………………………………………………..................

………………………………………………………………………………..................

………………………………………………………………………………..................

    Answer……………………………….   (3 marks)

14   The shape consists of two overlapping circles below. C_1 and C_2 are centres of the circles.

Find the perimeter of this shape.

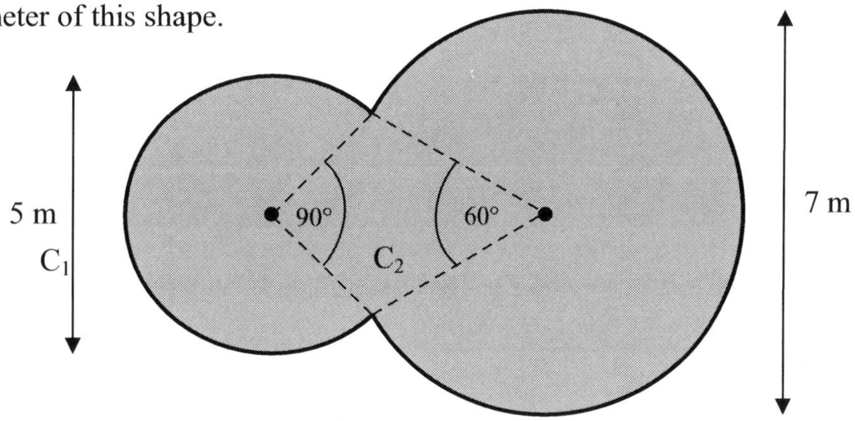

Give your answer in terms of π.

………………………………………………………………………………..................

………………………………………………………………………………..................

………………………………………………………………………………..................

………………………………………………………………………………..................

………………………………………………………………………………..................

    Answer……………………………….   (5 marks)

8

15   When I am at point A, the angle of elevation of the top of a tree T is $30°$, but if I walk 10 m towards the tree, to point B, the angle of elevation is then $45°$.

15(a)   Work out the height of the tree.

The height of the tree is x m

Give your answer in the form $a(b+\sqrt{3})$, where a and b are integers.

....

....

....

....

....

....

         Answer.................................   (3 marks)

15(b)   Work out the distance AT.

Give your answer in the form $a(b+\sqrt{3})$, where a and b are integers.

....

....

....

....

....

....

         Answer.................................   (3 marks)

16   The diagram shows a solid prism with the same cross-section through its length. The cross-section is a right-angled triangle with height 30 cm. The base ABCD is rectangle of width 20 cm and length 40 cm. The prism is made from wood with density 0.0005 kg/cm³.

Work out the mass of the prism.

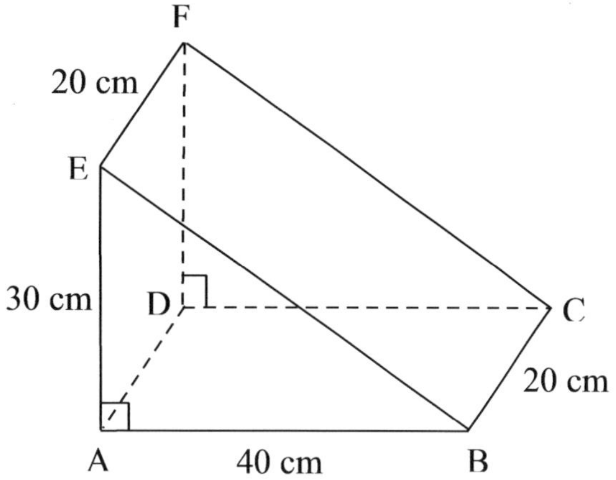

....

....

....

....

....

....

Answer................................   (4 marks)

17   The diagram, which is not drawn to scale, shows the graph of $y = 2^x$.

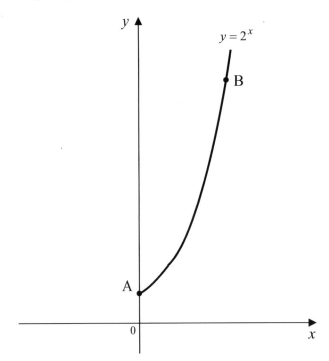

The points A(0, a) and B(3, b) lie on the curve.

17(a) Find the value of a and the value of b.

    ………………………………………………………………………………..................

    ………………………………………………………………………………..................

    ………………………………………………………………………………..................

         Answer……………………………….   (4 marks)

17(b) Add to the diagram to show the shape of the curve $y = 2^x$ for negative values of x.

    ………………………………………………………………………………..................

    ………………………………………………………………………………..................

    ………………………………………………………………………………..................

                                              (3 marks)

18(a)   On the diagram, draw the image of Shape A when it is reflected in the *x*-axis.

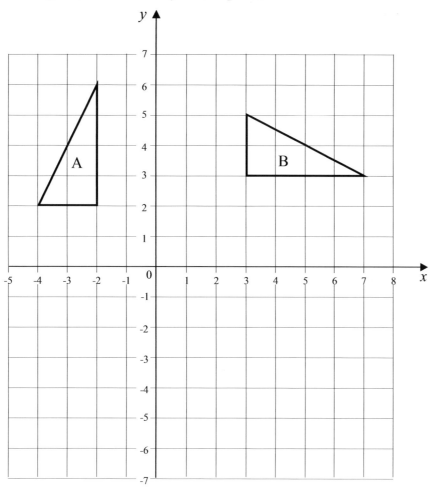

....

(3 marks)

18(b)   On the diagram, draw the image of Shape B when it is translated by the vector $\begin{pmatrix} -1 \\ -6 \end{pmatrix}$.

....

....

....

(3 marks)

18(c)   Describe fully the single transformation which will map Shape A onto Shape B.

....

....

(3 marks)

9

11

19   On the grid below indicate clearly the region R defined by the three inequalities.

$x \le 2$

$y \le x + 3$

$y \ge -x - 3$

19(a)   Label the region clearly with an R.

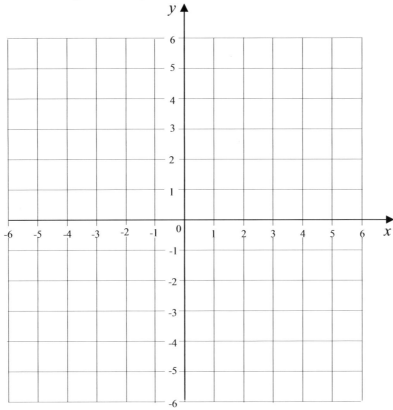

(3 marks)

19(b)   Calculate the area of the region R.

....

....

....

....

....

....

Answer............................   (3 marks)

6

20(a) Sketch the parabola of $y = \dfrac{1}{2}(x+3)^2 - 2$.

....

....

(3 marks)

20(b) On your sketch, show clearly the coordinates of the turning point.

....

....

(3 marks)

20(c) On your sketch, show clearly the coordinates of the points of intersection with the x-axis and y-axis.

....

....

(3 marks)

20(d) On your sketch, show clearly the line of symmetry.

....

....

(3 marks)

Paper 2 (Non-Calculator)

Materials
For this paper you must have:
- mathematical instruments

You **must** not use a calculator

Time allowed
1 hour 30 minutes.

Instructions
- Use black ink. Draw diagrams in HB pencil.
- Answer all questions.
- You must answer the questions in the space provided. Do not write outside the box around each page or on blank pages.
- Do all rough work in this book. Cross through any work that you do not want to be marked.
- In all calculations, show clearly how you work out your answer.

Information
- The marks for questions are shown in brackets.
- The maximum mark is 100.

Advice
- Read each question carefully before you start to answer it.
- Keep an eye on the time.
- Try to answer every question.
- Check your answers if you have time at the end.

1(a) Work out $2\frac{1}{6}+1\frac{3}{4}$

....

....

Answer............................. (3 marks)

1(b) Work out $2\frac{2}{3}\times1\frac{5}{7}$.

Give your answer as a mixed number in its simplest form.

....

....

Answer............................. (3 marks)

2 *a* is a positive integer, show that $\sqrt{2a}(\sqrt{8a}+a\sqrt{2a})$ is always a multiple of 2.

....

....

(3 marks)

3 Work out $5\times10^5+2.5\times10^4$

Give your answer in standard form.

....

....

Answer............................. (3 marks)

4 Here is the nutritional information for a 110g serving of cereal.

Carbohydrates 88.4g,   Proteins 9.5g,   Fats 1.1g,

Sugar 8.5g,   Fibre 2.5g

John says that more than 80% of this serving is carbohydrates. Is he correct? Explain your reasoning.

....

....

....

Answer............................. (4 marks)

16

5   P is directly proportional to Q^2 where $Q > 0$. $P = 400$ when $Q = 10$.

5(a)   Find a formula for P in terms of Q.

....

....

....

Answer…………………………   (3 marks)

5(b)   Find the value of Q when $P = 36$.

....

....

....

Answer…………………………   (3 marks)

6   John has some money. He spent one quarter of it on sweets. He spent half of the
remaining amount on juice. From the money he had left, he spent two thirds of it on a
comic. If he had £2.00 left, how much did he start with?

....

....

....

....

....

....

....

....

....

....

....

....

Answer…………………………   (4 marks)

7   A car leaves Birmingham New Street travelling 50 miles per hour. An hour later, a
     second car leaves Birmingham New Street following the first car, travelling 70
     miles per hour.

     How long will it take the second car to overtake the first car, after leaving

     Birmingham New Street?

     ....

     ....

     ....

          Answer.................................   (4 marks)

8   John says that $27^{-\frac{1}{3}} = \frac{1}{9}$

     Explain his error and give the correct value of $27^{-\frac{1}{3}}$ in the form $\frac{p}{q}$.

     ....

     ....

     ....

          Answer.................................   (3 marks)

9(a) Write $\frac{5}{9}$ as a recurring decimal.

     ....

     ....

     ....

          Answer.................................   (3 marks)

9(b) Convert $0.2\dot{1}$ to a fraction in its simplest form.

     ....

     ....

     ....

     ....

     ....

          Answer.................................   (3 marks)

10   Rationalise the denominator and simply fully $\dfrac{\sqrt{2}-1}{2-\sqrt{2}}$

....

....

....

Answer................................   (3 marks)

11    $3x^2 + bx + 6 \equiv a(x-3)^2 + c$.

Work out the values of a, b and c.

....

....

....

Answer................................   (3 marks)

12   In a car park, there are 60 cars. $\dfrac{3}{5}$ of the cars are blue and 25% of the cars are red.

How many cars are neither blue nor red?

....

....

....

Answer................................   (3 marks)

13   A box contains toy cars. Each car is red or black or blue.

Jack takes a car at random from the box.

The table shows the probabilities that Jack takes a red car or a blue car or a black car or silver.

Colour of car	Probability
red	0.50
blue	0.30
black	

13(a)   Work out the probability that Jack takes a black car.

....

....

....

....

....

Answer…………………………….   (3 marks)

13(b)   Jack adds 50 black cars into the box. The following table shows the probabilities that Jack takes a red car or a blue car or a black car after he adds 50 black cars into the box.

Colour of car	Probability
red	0.375
blue	0.225
black	0.40

Work out the total number of cars in the box originally.

....

....

....

....

Answer…………………………….   (4 marks)

14   The cumulative frequency table shows information about the height of 50 men.

Height (h cm)	Cumulative frequency
$150 < h \le 160$	5
$150 < h \le 170$	15
$150 < h \le 180$	35
$150 < h \le 190$	45
$150 < h \le 200$	50

14(a)   On the grid, draw a cumulative frequency graph for the table.

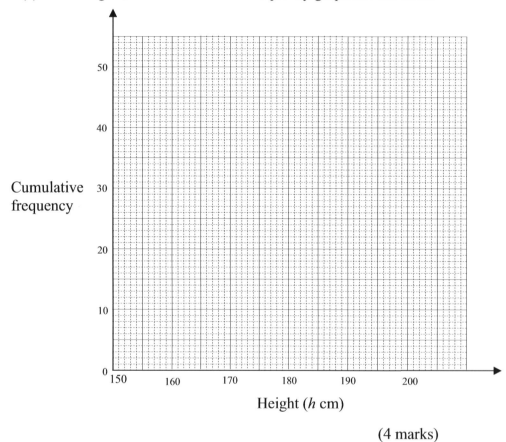

Height (h cm)

(4 marks)

14(b)   Use your graph to find an estimate for the median height of the 50 men.

....

....

....

        Answer................................   (3 marks)

14(c) Use your graph to find an estimate for the number of the men who are taller than 185 cm.

....

....

....

Answer……………………………. (3 marks)

15 In a regular polygon, the interior angle is seventeen times exterior angle, $x°$

15(a) Find the exterior angle

....

....

....

....

....

....

Answer……………………………. (4 marks)

15(b) Find the interior angle

....

....

....

Answer……………………………. (3 marks)

10

21

16   A, B, C and D are on the circumference of a circle, DT is a tangent to the circle at
      D.

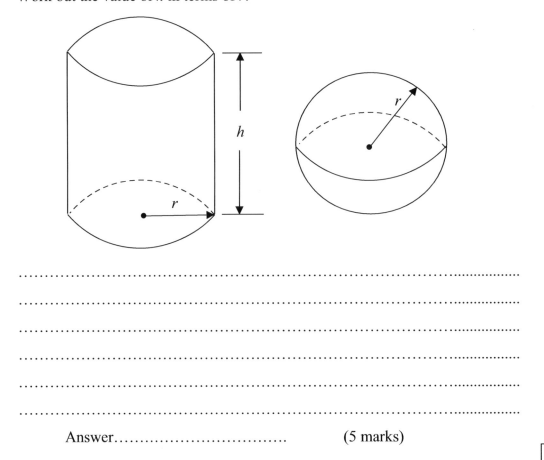

      Prove that triangle ADE is similar to triangle DBE.

      ………………………………………………………………………....…..

      ………………………………………………………………………....…..

      ………………………………………………………………………....…..

                                                              (4 marks)

17   The diagram shows a cylinder and a sphere. The base of the cylinder and the sphere
      have the same radius r cm. The ratio of their volumes, the cylinder: the sphere is 3:2.
      Work out the value of h in terms of r.

      ………………………………………………………………………….......

      ………………………………………………………………………….......

      ………………………………………………………………………….......

      ………………………………………………………………………….......

      ………………………………………………………………………….......

      ………………………………………………………………………….......

            Answer…………………………   (5 marks)

9

22

18   The diagram shows a circle, centre C. TP is a tangent to the circle and intersects the circle at P.

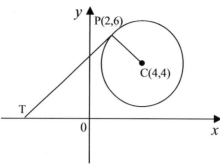

Work out the equation of line TP.

....

....

....

....

....

....

....

....

        Answer...............................   (4 marks)

4

23

19(a) Complete the table of values for $y = 6 + 2x - x^2$ and use it to draw the graph of $y = 6 + 2x - x^2$ for values of x from -3 to 4.

x	-3	-2	-1	0	1	2	3	4
y		-2	3	6		6	3	-2

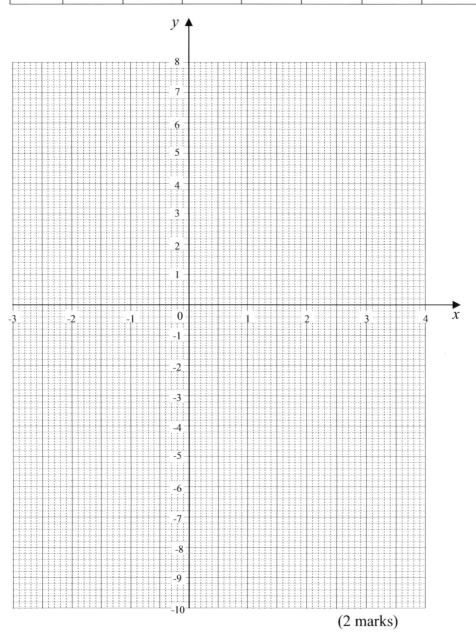

(2 marks)

19(b) On the same axes, draw the graph of the line $y = x + 3$

....

....

Answer………………………………   (2 marks)

4

19(c) Write down, correct to 1 decimal place, the coordinates of the point with a positive *x*-coordinate where the line meets the curve.

....

....

....

   Answer…………………………….   (3 marks)

20   The sketch shows $y = \sin x$ for $0° \le x \le 360°$

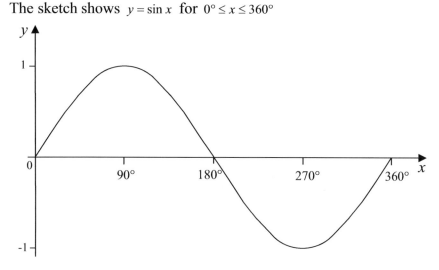

   The value of $\sin 25° = 0.423$ to 3 significant figures.

20(a) Use the sketch to find another angle between $0°$ and $360°$ for which $\sin x = 0.423$.

....

....

....

   Answer…………………………….   (4 marks)

20(b) Use the sketch to find out the value of $\sin 205°$.

....

....

....

   Answer…………………………….   (4 marks)

11

25

Paper 3 (Non-Calculator)

Materials

For this paper you must have:
- mathematical instruments

You **must** not use a calculator

Time allowed

1 hour 30 minutes.

Instructions

- Use black ink. Draw diagrams in HB pencil.
- Answer all questions.
- You must answer the questions in the space provided. Do not write outside the box around each page or on blank pages.
- Do all rough work in this book. Cross through any work that you do not want to be marked.
- In all calculations, show clearly how you work out your answer.

Information

- The marks for questions are shown in brackets.
- The maximum mark is 100.

Advice

- Read each question carefully before you start to answer it.
- Keep an eye on the time.
- Try to answer every question.
- Check your answers if you have time at the end.

1(a) Work out $2\frac{1}{6} - 1\frac{3}{4}$

....

....

....

Answer……………………………. (3 marks)

1(b) Work out $1\frac{3}{5} \div \frac{4}{7}$

Give your answer as a mixed number in its simplest form.

....

....

....

Answer……………………………. (3 marks)

2 Simplify $\dfrac{\sin 60° + \tan 30°}{\sin 45°}$

Give your answer in the form $\dfrac{a}{b}\sqrt{c}$,where a, b and c are integers

....

....

....

Answer……………………………. (3 marks)

3 n is an integer.

Prove $(n+4)^2 - (n+2)^2$ is divisible by 4.

....

....

....

(3 marks)

4   Jack's solution to the inequality $-x^2 - 2x + 15 > 0$ is shown on the number line.

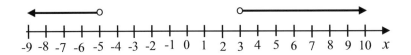

Is Jack's solution correct? Explain your reasoning.

……………………………………………………………………………………...............

……………………………………………………………………………………...............

……………………………………………………………………………………...............

……………………………………………………………………………………...............

……………………………………………………………………………………...............

(4 marks)

5   Chocolate bars are sold in two sizes. A standard bar costs 29p and weighs 50 g. A king-size bar costs 45p and weighs 75 g.

Which size of bar is the better value for money?

……………………………………………………………………………………...............

……………………………………………………………………………………...............

……………………………………………………………………………………...............

         Answer……………………………….   (4 marks)

6   y is inversely proportional to x.

Complete the table.

x	3	2	
y		6	24

……………………………………………………………………………………...............

……………………………………………………………………………………...............

……………………………………………………………………………………...............

(2 marks)

10

28

7   Rearrange $6 = \sqrt{\dfrac{wx}{x+w}}$ to make x the subject.

………………………………………………………………………………………....……

………………………………………………………………………………………....……

………………………………………………………………………………………....……

      Answer……………………………..   (3 marks)

8   a, b, c and d are four integers.

      Their mean is 50, their modal is 51, and their range is 10.

8(a)   Find the value of the largest of the four integers.

………………………………………………………………………….....…………

………………………………………………………………………….....…………

………………………………………………………………………….....…………

      Answer……………………………..   (4 marks)

8(b)   Find the mean value of the numbers $(2a\text{-}4)$, $(2b\text{-}4)$, $(2c\text{-}4)$ and $(2d\text{-}4)$.

………………………………………………………………………….....…………

………………………………………………………………………….....…………

………………………………………………………………………….....…………

      Answer……………………………..   (4 marks)

9(a)   Write $\dfrac{1}{9}$ as a recurring decimal

………………………………………………………………………….....…………

………………………………………………………………………….....…………

………………………………………………………………………….....…………

      Answer……………………………..   (3 marks)

9(b)   Write $3.0\dot{9}$ as a mixed number in its simplest form.

………………………………………………………………………….....…………

………………………………………………………………………….....…………

………………………………………………………………………….....…………

      Answer……………………………..   (4 marks)

18

10(a) Solve $x^3 = x(2x+3)$

....

....

....

Answer…………………………….   (3 marks)

10(b) Solve $\sqrt{12} + \sqrt{48} = \sqrt{27} + \sqrt{x}$

....

....

....

Answer…………………………….   (3 marks)

11    $f(x) = 16 - x^2 - 2x$ for all real values of x.

Solve $f(2x) = 8$

....

....

....

Answer…………………………….   (2 marks)

12   A parabola has a equation $y = x^2 + 4x + 5$.

Prove that the parabola does not intersect the x-axis

....

....

....

(3 marks)

13   All 25 pupils in John's class took a Maths test.

John calculated that the mean mark for the class was 40.0 marks. He calculated that the median mark was 38 marks.

After John had done the calculations, Emma found that John had not given the mark in her answer to Question 4.

John awarded Emma an extra 10 marks.

13(a)   Calculate the new mean mark for the class.

....

....

....

Answer……………………………   (3 marks)

Before Emma was awarded the extra marks, Emma had the fifth highest mark in the class.

13(b)   What is the effect of Emma's extra marks on the median mark? Does it increase, decrease or stay the same?

Explain your answer.

....

....

....

Answer……………………………   (3 marks)

14   The scatter graph shows the heights of boys at different ages.

14(a) Draw a line of best fit on the scatter graph.   (3 marks)

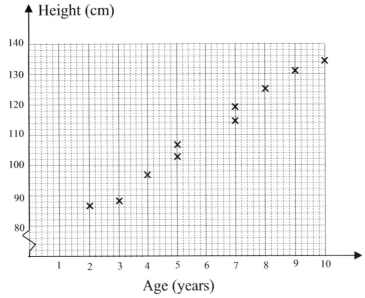

Age (years)

……………………………………………………………………………………

……………………………………………………………………………………

14(b) What type of correlation is there between age and height?

……………………………………………………………………………………

……………………………………………………………………………………

(3 marks)

14(c) Estimate the height of a six year old.

……………………………………………………………………………………

……………………………………………………………………………………

……………………………………………………………………………………

        Answer…………………………….   (3 marks)

15   There are 7 blue marbles and 3 red marbles in a bag. Two marbles are taken at random from the bag.

15(a)   Calculate, as an exactly fraction, the probability that two marbles are different colour.

....

....

....

....

       Answer…………………………….   (5 marks)

15(b)   Calculate, as an exactly fraction, the probability that both marbles are the same colour.

....

....

....

....

       Answer…………………………….   (5 marks)

16   QPRS is a cyclic quadrilateral. PS is a diameter.

Work out the value of x.

....

....

....

....

....

....

       Answer…………………………….   (5 marks)

17   The square ABCD is drawn inside the regular octagon ABEFGHIJ. They share side AB.

Work out the value of *x*.

....

....

....

Answer…………………………….   (5 marks)

18   This shape consists of a sector of a circle with 2 identical right-angled triangles.

Calculate the area of this shape.

Give your answer in terms of π.

....

....

....

....

....

....

Answer…………………………….   (5 marks)

19   The graph of $y = a\cos(x + b^\circ)$, $0^\circ \le x < 360^\circ$, $a > 0$, $-180 < b < 180$, is shown below.

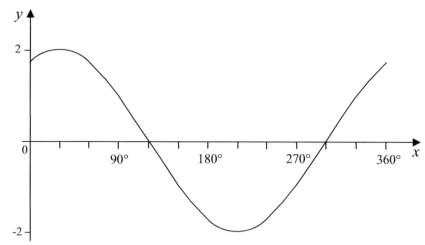

State the values of a and b.

……………………………………………………………………………………..............

……………………………………………………………………………………..............

……………………………………………………………………………………..............

        Answer…………………………….   (4 marks)

20   The sketch shows part of a circle, and a line $y = -2x + 6$. The line passes the centre

of the circle. The circle intersects the y-axis at points A and B.

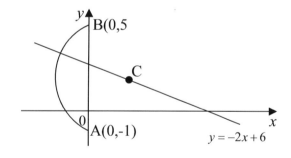

Work out the equation of the circle.

……………………………………………………………………………………..............

……………………………………………………………………………………..............

……………………………………………………………………………………..............

……………………………………………………………………………………..............

……………………………………………………………………………………..............

……………………………………………………………………………………..............

……………………………………………………………………………………..............

        Answer…………………………….   (5 marks)

9

Paper 4 (Non-Calculator)

Materials

For this paper you must have:
- mathematical instruments

You **must** not use a calculator

Time allowed

1 hour 30 minutes.

Instructions
- Use black ink. Draw diagrams in HB pencil.
- Answer all questions.
- You must answer the questions in the space provided. Do not write outside the box around each page or on blank pages.
- Do all rough work in this book. Cross through any work that you do not want to be marked.
- In all calculations, show clearly how you work out your answer.

Information
- The marks for questions are shown in brackets.
- The maximum mark is 100.

Advice
- Read each question carefully before you start to answer it.
- Keep an eye on the time.
- Try to answer every question.
- Check your answers if you have time at the end.

1   Work out

1(a) $\begin{pmatrix} 2 \\ 5 \end{pmatrix} + 3\begin{pmatrix} 5 \\ 3 \end{pmatrix}$

....

....

....

        Answer…………………………….   (3 marks)

1(b) $2\begin{pmatrix} 4 \\ 3 \end{pmatrix} - 4\begin{pmatrix} 3 \\ 5 \end{pmatrix}$

....

....

....

        Answer…………………………….   (3 marks)

2   Express $\sqrt{40} + 4\sqrt{10} + \sqrt{90}$ as a surd in its simplest form.

....

....

        Answer…………………………….   (3 marks)

3(a)   John drives 214 miles in 4 hours 53 minutes.

        Do a calculation to find an approximate value for his average speed.

....

....

....

        Answer…………………………….   (3 marks)

3(b)   Is your approximate value greater or less than John's actual average speed?

        Explain your answer.

....

....

        Answer…………………………….   (3 marks)

15

4 In a tennis club, $\frac{3}{5}$ of the members are women, $\frac{1}{4}$ of the members are men, and the rest of the members are children.

4(a) What percentage of the members are children?

....

....

Answer................................   (3 marks)

4(b) Find the ration women : children

....

....

....

Answer................................   (3 marks)

4(c) There are 15 children in the club, find the total number of members in the club.

....

....

....

....

Answer................................   (3 marks)

5(a) Fully factorise $(x^2 - 9) - (x - 3)(3x + 5)$

....

....

....

Answer................................   (3 marks)

5(b) By factorising fully, simplify $\dfrac{x^4 - 4x^3 + 3x^2}{x^4 - 10x^2 + 9}$

....

....

....

Answer................................   (3 marks)

6   A bus has some passengers on board at starting station. At the first stop two fifths get off and then 7 people get on. At the next stop a quarter of the people remaining on the bus get off and then 13 get on. There are 34 passengers on board now. How many passengers are there on the bus at starting station?

....

....

....

        Answer................................   (3 marks)

7(a)   Expand and simplify $(2x+3y)(3x-2y)$

....

....

....

        Answer................................   (3 marks)

7(b)   Write as a single fraction $\dfrac{6}{x^2-9}-\dfrac{1}{x-3}$

        Give your answer in its simplest form.

....

....

....

        Answer................................   (3 marks)

8   a, b, c and d are consecutive integers.

     Explain why $(a+b)(c+d)$ is always odd.

....

....

....

....

....

....

                                        (4 marks)

13

9　You are given that $5.6 \times 13.2 = 73.92$ exactly.

9(a)　Emma says that $56 \times 0.0132 = 7.392$

Without doing an exact calculation, show that Emma is wrong.

....

....

....

....

....

....

(3 marks)

9(b)　Find the exact value of 0.056×132

....

....

....

Answer................................　(3 marks)

10　$x : y = 3 : 4$ and z is 20% of y.

Work out $x : y : z$

Give your answer in its simplest form.

....

....

....

....

....

....

Answer................................　(3 marks)

11   The four candidates in an election were A, B, C and D.

The pie chart shows the proportion of votes for each candidate.

Work out the probability that a person who voted, chosen at random, voted for A.

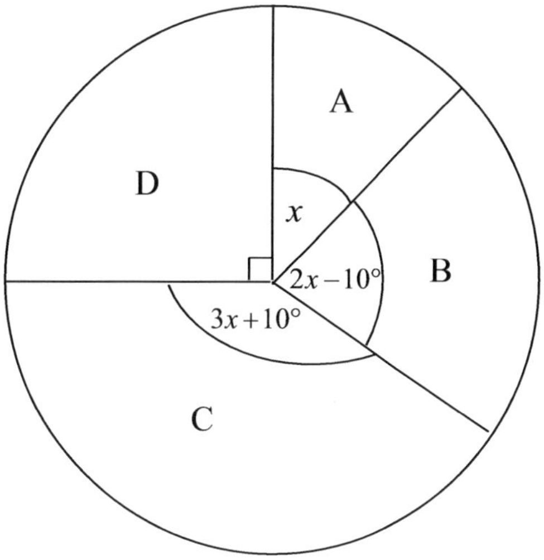

....

....

....

Answer................................   (4 marks)

12   There are

8 different sandwiches

5 different drinks

and

3 different snacks.

| **Meal Deal** |
| Choose one sandwich, one drink and one snack |

12(a) How many different Meal Deal combinations are there?

....

....

....

Answer................................   (3 marks)

12(b)   Two of the sandwiches have cheese in them.

Three of the drinks are fizzy.

Emma picks a Meal Deal at random.

Work out the probability that the sandwich has cheese in it and the drink is fizzy.

Give your answer as a fraction in its simplest form.

....

....

....

Answer................................   (3 marks)

13   Emma is a member of a video club.

She pays a fixed charge of £20 every six months.

She pays an additional charge for every video she hires.

The line on the graph shows cost for six months to Emma for up to 20 videos hired.

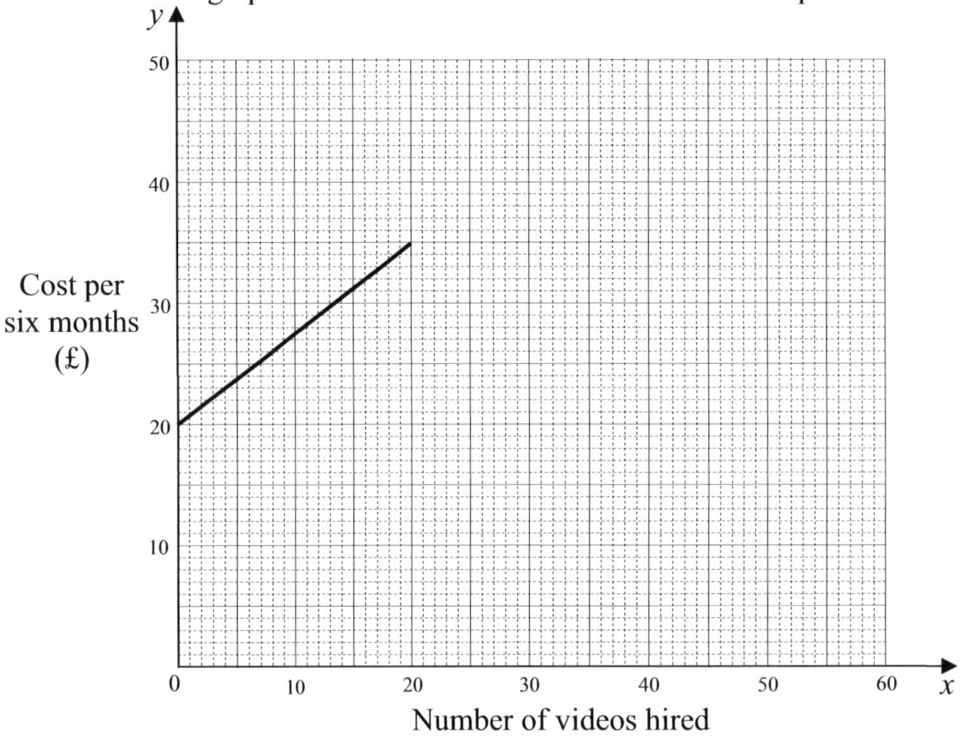

13(a)   Calculate the cost of hiring each of the first 20 videos.

....

....

....

Answer................................   (3 marks)

6

Once she has hired 20 videos in any six month period, she pays only 50p for every additional video she hires.

13(b) Draw a line on the graph so that the graph can be used to calculate the total cost in a six-month period of hiring up to 50 videos.

…………………………………………………………………………..................

…………………………………………………………………………..................

…………………………………………………………………………..................

(3 marks)

14   Two congruent regular polygons are joined together.

Diagram **NOT**
accurately

30°

Work out the number of sides on each polygon.

……………………………………………………………………….........................

……………………………………………………………………….........................

……………………………………………………………………….........................

……………………………………………………………………….........................

……………………………………………………………………….........................

……………………………………………………………………….........................

Answer………………………….   (3 marks)

15   In the diagram shown below:

ABE is a tangent to the circle with centre O

$\angle DBE = 58°$

Calculate $\angle CAB$.

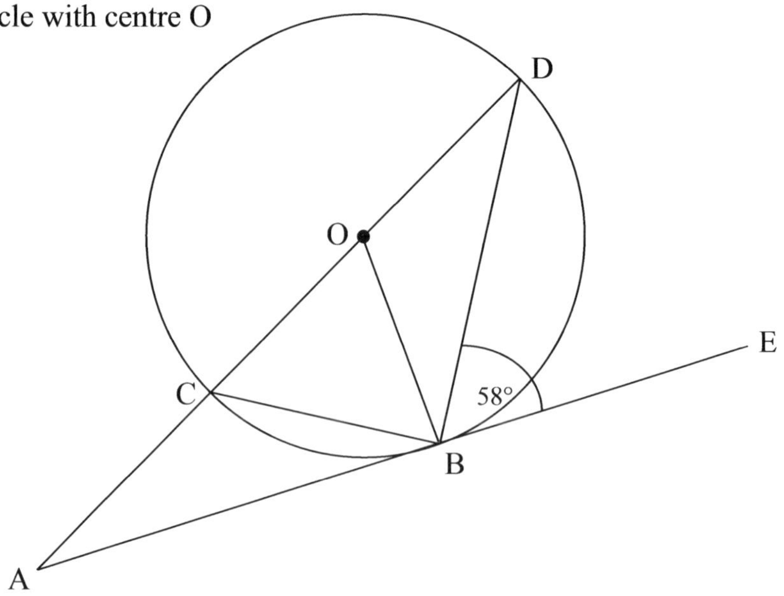

....

....

....

....

....

....

....

....

Answer…………………………….   (3 marks)

16   A rectangle has a length of x cm and a width of y cm.

x cm

y cm

The rectangle has a perimeter of 13 cm and an area of 10 cm^2.

16(a) Show that $2x^2 - 13x + 20 = 0$

....

....

....

....

....

....

                                                                (3 marks)

16(b) Solve the equation $2x^2 - 13x + 20 = 0$

....

....

....

         Answer................................   (2 marks)

5

17   The vectors **p** and **q** are shown in the diagram below.

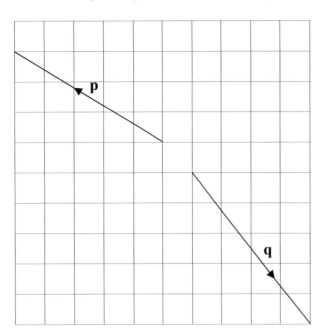

17(a)   Draw **v** = **p** + **q**.

....

....

....

....

....

....

(3 marks)

17(b)   Draw **w** = **p** - **q**.

....

....

....

....

....

....

(3 marks)

18   The line L_1 in the diagram has a gradient of 3, and it passes through the point $(0, 2)$.

The line L_2 is perpendicular to L_1 and also passes through the point $(0, 2)$.

Find the equation of the line L_2.

Give your answer in the form $y = mx + b$

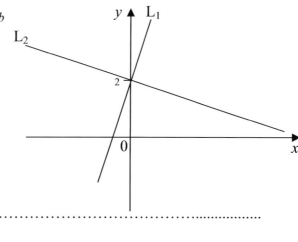

....

....

Answer………………………….   (3 marks)

19   David invests money into an account which pays a fixed rate of compound interest each year. The value, £P, of his investment after t years is given by the formula

$P = 15000 \times 1.05^t$

19(a)   How much money did David invest?

....

Answer………………………….   (2 marks)

19(b)   What rate of compound interest is paid each year?

....

Answer………………………….   (2 marks)

19(c)   Which graph is the best to represent the growth in David's account?

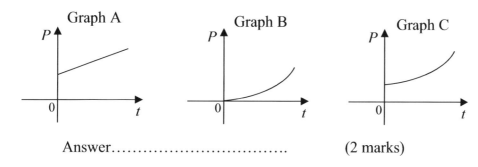

Answer………………………….   (2 marks)

9

20   A flea jumps from point A and lands at point B. Its path is that of a parabola with

equation $y = \dfrac{-x^2 + 6x + 16}{2}$, where x is the horizontal distance travelled and y is its

height. All measurements are in centimetres.

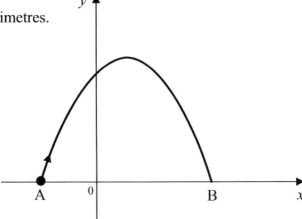

20(a) Calculate how far the flea has travelled horizontally from A to B.

....

....

....

        Answer……………………………….   (3 marks)

20(b) Calculate the maximum height reached by the flea during its jump.

....

....

....

        Answer……………………………….   (3 marks)

6

Paper 1 solutions

1(a)   Work out $(2+\sqrt{3})(2-\sqrt{3})$

$(2+\sqrt{3})(2-\sqrt{3})=2^2-(\sqrt{3})^2=4-3=1$

Answer   1   (3 marks)

1(b)   Without using a calculator, work out $\dfrac{\sqrt{32}+\sqrt{50}}{\sqrt{18}}$

Show all your working.

$\dfrac{\sqrt{32}+\sqrt{50}}{\sqrt{18}}=\dfrac{4\sqrt{2}+5\sqrt{2}}{3\sqrt{2}}=3$

Answer   3   (3 marks)

2   By writing each number correct to 1 significant figure, find an approximate value

for $\dfrac{\sqrt{9.115}\times10^5}{5.997\times10^{-4}}$

Give your answer in standard form.

$\dfrac{\sqrt{9.115}\times10^5}{5.997\times10^{-4}}\approx\dfrac{3\times10^5}{6\times10^{-4}}=0.5\times10^9=5\times10^8$

Answer 5×10^8 (3 marks)

3   Average speed $=\dfrac{\text{distance}}{\text{time}}$

If the distance is doubled and the time is halved, what happens to the average speed?

Circle your answer.

×2   ×4   no change   ÷2   ÷4

Answer   ×4   (3 marks)

12

49

4   Jack received 25% more emails in December than in November. Jack received 250 emails in December. How many more emails did Jack receive in December than in November?

In November, the number of emails which Jack received: $\dfrac{250}{1+25\%}$

$250 - \dfrac{250}{1+25\%} = 250 - 200 = 50$

Answer   50   (3 marks)

5   A plant is 6 cm high and growing at a steady rate of 0.2 cm every day.

5(a)   After how many days will the height reach 11 cm?

$6 + 0.2x = 11 \Rightarrow x = \dfrac{11-6}{0.2} = 25$

Answer   25 days   (3 marks)

5(b)   If the plant is growing at a slower rate, what effect will this have on your answer to part (a)?

Answer   it would take more days   (3 marks)

6   Jack is making some small snacks for a party. He cuts 1.2 kg of cheese into a number of 15g pieces. How many pieces does he have?

Jack says

I can cut it into 80 pieces.

Is he correct? Show how you decide.

$\dfrac{1200}{15} = 80$

Answer   yes, he is correct   (3 marks)

7   Rearrange $\dfrac{1}{x} + \dfrac{1}{y} = \dfrac{1}{w}$ to make y the subject.

$\dfrac{1}{x} + \dfrac{1}{y} = \dfrac{1}{w} \Rightarrow \dfrac{1}{y} = \dfrac{x-w}{xw} \Rightarrow x = \dfrac{xw}{x-w}$

Answer $y = \dfrac{xw}{x-w}$ (3 marks)

15

8   The price of a television is reduced by 30% for a sale.

Afterwards, the sale price is increased by 40%.

Jack says the television is now 10% more expensive than before the sale.

Explain Jack's error and work out the correct percentage change in the price of the television from before the sale to after the sale.

$(1-30\%)(1+40\%)-1=0.7\times1.4-1=0.98-1=-0.02=-2\%$

Answer   decrease of 2%   (3 marks)

9   The first four terms of a sequence are

2   8   32   128

9(a)   Work out the next term.

$\dfrac{a_n}{a_{n-1}}=4$, where $n\geq2$

$a_5=4a_4=4\times128=512$

Answer   512   (3 marks)

9(b)   Find the nth term.

$a_n=2\times4^{n-1}$

Answer $2\times4^{n-1}$ (3 marks)

10   There are 9 counters in a bag.

There is a number on each counter.

Jack takes at random 2 counters from the bag.

He adds together the numbers on the 2 counters to get his Total.

10(a)   Complete and fully label the probability tree diagram to show the possible outcome.

First counter   Second counter

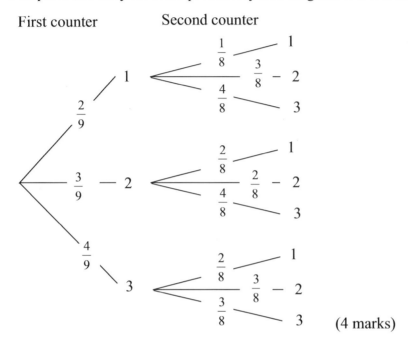

(4 marks)

10(b)   Work out the probability that his Total is greater than 3.

Give your answer as a fraction in its simplest form.

From the probability tree diagram, the probability, that his Total is greater than 3,

can be calculated as follows.

$$\frac{2}{9} \times \frac{4}{8} + \frac{3}{9} \times (\frac{2}{8} + \frac{4}{8}) + \frac{4}{9} = \frac{29}{36}$$

Answer $\frac{29}{36}$ (2 marks)

6

11   The table shows information about the number of fish caught by 29 people in a club in one day.

Jack is one of the 29 people in the club.

Number of fish	Frequency
0	2
1	6
2	10
3	8
5	2
8	1

The number of fish caught by him was the same as the median number of fish caught for his club.

Work out the number of fish caught by him.

$\frac{29+1}{2}=15$, Jack is in the 15th position for the number of fish caught for his club, so that the number of fish caught by him is 2.

Answer   2   (3 marks)

12   The diagram below is made from three squares.

Find the ratio

total shaded area : total unshaded area.

Give your answer in the simplest form.

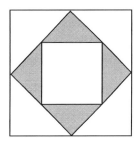

The ratio of the side of three squares is as follows:

smallest: median: largest $= 1 : \sqrt{2} : 2$

∴ total shaded area : total unshaded area $= [(\sqrt{2})^2 - 1^2] : [2^2 - (\sqrt{2})^2 + 1^2] = 1 : 3$

Answer   1:3   (3 marks)

6

(Alternative method:

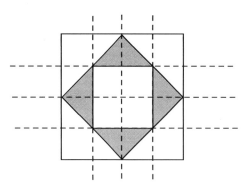

Draw the dotted lines to divide the largest square into 16 portions. The shaded contains 4 portions. The unshaded contains 12 portions

total shaded area : total unshaded area $= 4:12 = 1:3$)

13   Points A, B, C and D are on the circumference of a circle. AE is a tangent to the circle.

Work out $\angle ACD$

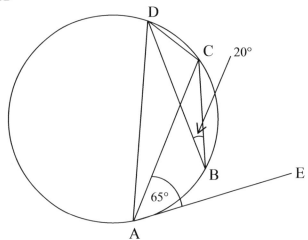

Points A, B, C and D are on the circumference of a circle, $\therefore \ \angle CAD = \angle CBD = 20°$,

AE is a tangent to the circle, $\therefore \ \angle CDA = \angle CAE = 65°$

In triangle ACD, $\angle ACD = 180° - \angle CAD - \angle CDA = 180° - 20° - 65° = 95°$

    Answer   95°   (3 marks)

3

14   The shape consists of two overlapping circles below. C_1 and C_2 are centres of the circles.

Find the perimeter of this shape.

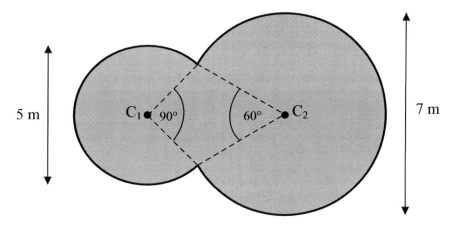

Give your answer in terms of π.

$$(1-\frac{90°}{360°})\times\pi\times5+(1-\frac{60°}{360°})\times\pi\times7=\frac{3}{4}\times\pi\times5+\frac{5}{6}\times\pi\times7=\frac{115}{12}\pi$$

Answer $\frac{115}{12}\pi$ m   (5 marks)

15   When I am at point A, the angle of elevation of the top of a tree T is $30°$, but if I walk 10 m towards the tree, to point B, the angle of elevation is then $45°$.

15(a) Work out the height of the tree.

The height of the tree is x m

Give your answer in the form $a(b+\sqrt{3})$, where a and b are integers.

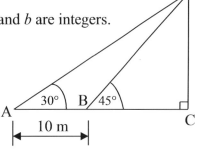

$$(AB+BC)^2 + TC^2 = AT^2 \Rightarrow (10+x)^2 + x^2 = (\frac{x}{\sin 30°})^2$$

$x = 5 \pm 5\sqrt{3}$

Clearly a negative answer is not suitable here, so that the height of the tree is $5(1+\sqrt{3})$ m.

Answer $5(1+\sqrt{3})$ m   (3 marks)

8

15(b) Work out the distance AT.

Give your answer in the form $a(b+\sqrt{3})$, where a and b are integers.

$$AT = \frac{TC}{\sin 30°} = \frac{5(1+\sqrt{3})}{\frac{1}{2}} = 10(1+\sqrt{3})$$

Answer $10(1+\sqrt{3})\,\text{m}$ (3 marks)

16 The diagram shows a solid prism with the same cross-section through its length. The cross-section is a right-angled triangle with height 30 cm. The base ABCD is rectangle of width 20 cm and length 40 cm. The prism is made from wood with density 0.0005 kg/cm³.

Work out the mass of the prism.

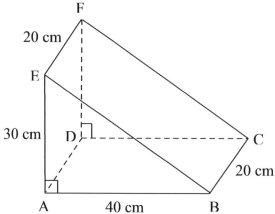

The prism has a height of 20 cm and the cross section with the right-angled triangle.

The volume of the prism is:

$$\frac{AB \times AE}{2} \times BC$$

∴ The mass of the prism is

$$\frac{AB \times AE}{2} \times BC \times 0.0005 = \frac{40 \times 30}{2} \times 20 \times 0.0005 = 6$$

Answer   6 kg   (4 marks)

7

17   The diagram, which is not drawn to scale, shows the graph of $y = 2^x$.

The points A(0, a) and B(3, b) lie on the curve.

17(a) Find the value of a and the value of b.

$y = 2^x \Rightarrow a = 2^0 = 1$, $b = 2^3 = 8$

Answer $a = 1$, $b = 8$ (4 marks)

17(b) Add to the diagram to show the shape of the curve $y = 2^x$ for negative values of x.

As shown on the diagram.

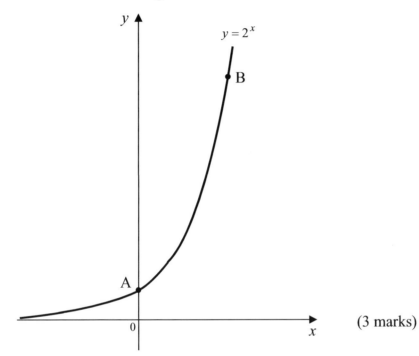

(3 marks)

18(a) On the diagram, draw the image of Shape A when it is reflected in the *x*-axis.

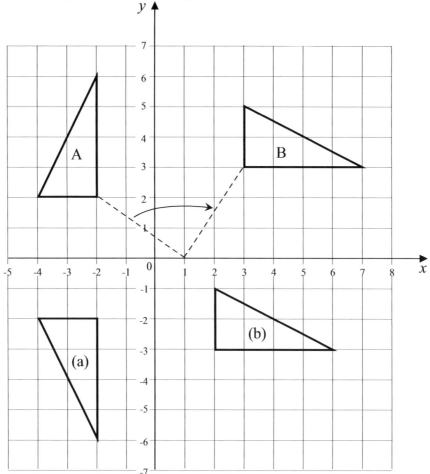

As shown on the diagram. (3 marks)

18(b) On the diagram, draw the image of Shape B when it is translated by the vector $\begin{pmatrix} -1 \\ -6 \end{pmatrix}$.

As shown on the diagram. (3 marks)

18(c) Describe fully the single transformation which will map Shape A onto Shape B.

Rotation 90° clockwise about (1,0). (3 marks)

19   On the grid below indicate clearly the region *R* defined by the three inequalities.

$x \leq 2$

$y \leq x + 3$

$y \geq -x - 3$

19(a) Label the region clearly with an R.

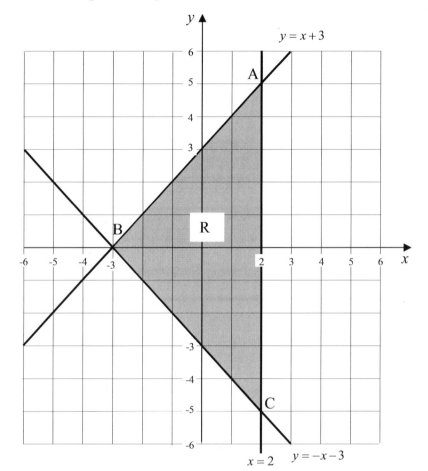

As shown on the diagram.   (3 marks)

19(b) Calculate the area of the region R.

The area of the region $R = \dfrac{(A_y - C_y)(A_x - B_x)}{2} = \dfrac{(5+5)(2+3)}{2} = 25$

Answer   25 square units.   (3 marks)

20(a)   Sketch the parabola of $y = \frac{1}{2}(x+3)^2 - 2$.   (3 marks)

As shown on the diagram below.

20(b)   On your sketch, show clearly the coordinates of the turning point.
The coordinates of the turning point are (-3, -2), as shown on the sketch below.

(3 marks)

20(c)   On your sketch, show clearly the coordinates of the points of intersection with the
x-axis and y-axis.

$x = 0, \; y = \frac{1}{2} \times 3^2 - 2 = 2.5$; $y = 0, \; x = -3 \pm 2 \Rightarrow x = -1, \; x = -5 \;$ from $\; y = \frac{1}{2}(x+3)^2 - 2$.

The coordinates of the points of intersection with the x-axis are (-1, 0) and (-5,0).
The coordinates of the points of intersection with the y-axis are (0, 2.5), as shown
on the diagram below.   (3 marks)

20(d)   On your sketch, show clearly the line of symmetry.
The equation of the line of symmetry is $x = -3$, and the line of symmetry is shown
on the diagram.

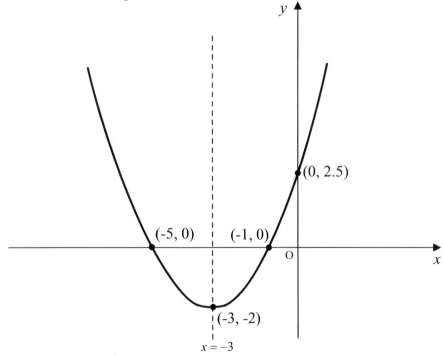

(3 marks)

12

60

Paper 2 solutions

1(a)   Work out $2\frac{1}{6} + 1\frac{3}{4}$

$$2\frac{1}{6} + 1\frac{3}{4} = 2\frac{2}{12} + 1\frac{9}{12} = 3\frac{11}{12}$$

Answer $3\frac{11}{12}$ (3 marks)

1(b)   Work out $2\frac{2}{3} \times 1\frac{5}{7}$.

Give your answer as a mixed number in its simplest form.

$$2\frac{2}{3} \times 1\frac{5}{7} = \frac{8}{\cancel{3}_1} \times \frac{\cancel{12}^{4}}{7} = \frac{32}{7} = 4\frac{4}{7}$$

Answer $4\frac{4}{7}$ (3 marks)

2   a is a positive integer, show that $\sqrt{2a}(\sqrt{8a} + a\sqrt{2a})$ is always a multiple of 2.

$$\sqrt{2a}(\sqrt{8a} + a\sqrt{2a}) = \sqrt{2a}(2\sqrt{2a} + a\sqrt{2a}) = 4a + 2a^2 = 2(2a + a^2)$$

$\therefore \sqrt{2a}(\sqrt{8a} + a\sqrt{2a})$ is always a multiple of 2   (3 marks)

3   Work out $5 \times 10^5 + 2.5 \times 10^4$

Give your answer in standard form.

$$5 \times 10^5 + 2.5 \times 10^4 = 5 \times 10^5 + 0.25 \times 10^5 = 5.25 \times 10^5$$

Answer 5.25×10^5 (3 marks)

4   Here is the nutritional information for a 110g serving of cereal.

Carbohydrates 88.4g,   Proteins 9.5g

Fats 1.1g,   Sugar 8.5g

Fibre 2.5g

John says that more than 80% of this serving is carbohydrates. Is he correct? Explain your reasoning.

$$\frac{88.4}{110} \times 100\% > \frac{88}{110} \times 100\% - 80\% \Rightarrow \frac{88.4}{110} \times 100\% > 80\%$$

Answer   Yes, he is correct.   (4 marks)

16

61

5   P is directly proportional to Q^2 where $Q > 0$. $P = 400$ when $Q = 10$.

5(a)   Find a formula for P in terms of Q.

$P = kQ^2$ where k is a constant.

$k = \dfrac{P}{Q^2} = \dfrac{400}{10^2} = 4$, $\therefore P = 4Q^2$

Answer $P = 4Q^2$ (3 marks)

5(b)   Find the value of Q when $P = 36$.

$P = 4Q^2 \Rightarrow Q = \pm\sqrt{\dfrac{P}{4}}$

$Q > 0$, clearly the negative answer is not suitable here. $Q = \sqrt{\dfrac{P}{4}} = \sqrt{\dfrac{36}{4}} = 3$

Answer   3   (3 marks)

6   John has some money. He spent one quarter of it on sweets. He spent half of the remaining amount on juice. From the money he had left, he spent two thirds of it on a comic. If he had £2.00 left, how much did he start with?

From the money he had left, he spent two thirds of it on a comic, and he had £2.00 left.

It means that he spent £4.00 on a comic ($\dfrac{2}{3} \times 6 = 4$). He had £6.00 left before he spent the money on a comic.

He spent half of the remaining amount on juice. It means that he spent £6.00 on juice. He had £12.00 before he spent the money on juice.

He spent one quarter of it on sweets, it means that $\dfrac{3}{4}x = 12 \Rightarrow x = 16$ if he started with £x.

        Answer   £16.00   (4 marks)

(Alternative method: if he started with x, then

sweets: $\dfrac{x}{4}$,   juice: $\dfrac{x - \dfrac{x}{4}}{2} = \dfrac{3x}{8}$,   a comic: $\dfrac{2}{3}(x - \dfrac{x}{4} - \dfrac{3x}{8}) = \dfrac{x}{4}$

$\dfrac{x}{4} + \dfrac{3x}{8} + \dfrac{x}{4} + 2 = x \Rightarrow x = 16$)

10

7 A car leaves Birmingham New Street travelling 50 miles per hour. An hour later, a second car leaves Birmingham New Street following the first car, travelling 70 miles per hour.

How long will it take the second car to overtake the first car, after leaving Birmingham New Street?

The second car takes x hours to overtake the first car, after leaving Birmingham New Street.

$x \times 70 = (x+1) \times 50 \Rightarrow 70x - 50x = 50 \Rightarrow x = 2.5$

Answer   2.5 hours   (4 marks)

8 John says that $27^{-\frac{1}{3}} = \frac{1}{9}$

Explain his error and give the correct value of $27^{-\frac{1}{3}}$ in the form $\frac{p}{q}$.

He divided by 3 and did not cube root. $27^{-\frac{1}{3}} = \frac{1}{\sqrt[3]{27}} = \frac{1}{3}$

Answer $\frac{1}{3}$ (3 marks)

9(a) Write $\frac{5}{9}$ as a recurring decimal.

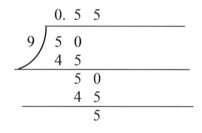

Answer $0.\dot{5}$ (3 marks)

9(b) Convert $0.\dot{2}\dot{1}$ to a fraction in its simplest form.

$x = 0.\dot{2}\dot{1}$ (1)

$100x = 21.\dot{2}\dot{1}$ (2)

Eq. (2) – Eq. (1) $99x = 21 \Rightarrow x = \frac{21}{99} = \frac{7}{33}$

Answer $\frac{7}{33}$ (3 marks)

13

10   Rationalise the denominator and simply fully $\dfrac{\sqrt{2}-1}{2-\sqrt{2}}$

$$\frac{\sqrt{2}-1}{2-\sqrt{2}} = \frac{(\sqrt{2}-1)(2+\sqrt{2})}{(2-\sqrt{2})(2+\sqrt{2})} = \frac{2\sqrt{2}+2-2-\sqrt{2}}{2} = \frac{\sqrt{2}}{2}$$

        Answer $\dfrac{\sqrt{2}}{2}$ (3 marks)

11     $3x^2 + bx + 6 \equiv a(x-3)^2 + c$.

    Work out the values of a, b and c.

$$3x^2 + bx + 6 = 3(x+\frac{b}{6})^2 - \frac{b^2}{12} + 6$$

$$a=3 ,\ \frac{b}{6} = -3 \Rightarrow b = -18 ,\ -\frac{b^2}{12} + 6 = c \Rightarrow c = -21$$

        Answer $a=3$, $b=-18$, $c=-21$ (3 marks)

12   In a car park, there are 60 cars. $\dfrac{3}{5}$ of the cars are blue and 25% of the cars are red.

    How many cars are neither blue nor red?

$$60 \times (1 - \frac{3}{5} - 25\%) = 60 \times 0.15 = 9$$

        Answer   9   (3 marks)

9

13 A box contains toy cars. Each car is red or black or blue.

Jack takes a car at random from the box.

The table shows the probabilities that Jack takes a red car or a blue car or a black car or silver.

Colour of car	Probability
red	0.50
blue	0.30
black	

13(a) Work out the probability that Jack takes a black car.

The probability that Jack takes a black car is:

$1 - 0.50 - 0.30 = 0.2$

Answer   0.2   (3 marks)

13(b) Jack adds 50 black cars into the box. The following table shows the probabilities that Jack takes a red car or a blue car or a black car after he adds 50 black cars into the box.

Colour of car	Probability
red	0.375
blue	0.225
black	0.40

Work out the total number of cars in the box originally.

The total number of cars in the box originally is x

$0.4(x + 50) - 0.2x = 50 \Rightarrow x = 150$

Answer   150   (4 marks)

14   The cumulative frequency table shows information about the height of 50 men.

Height (*h* cm)	Cumulative frequency
$150 < h \leq 160$	5
$150 < h \leq 170$	15
$150 < h \leq 180$	35
$150 < h \leq 190$	45
$150 < h \leq 200$	50

14(a)   On the grid, draw a cumulative frequency graph for the table.

As shown on the diagram.

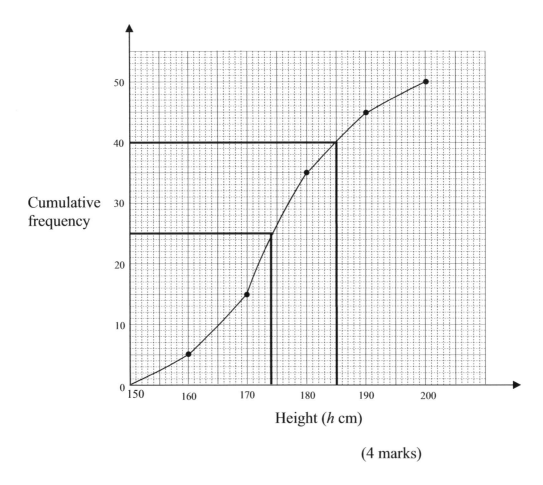

(4 marks)

14(b)   Use your graph to find an estimate for the median height of the 50 men.

174 cm, as shown on the diagram.

Answer   174 cm   (3 marks)

7

66

14(c) Use your graph to find an estimate for the number of the men who are taller than 185 cm.

From the cumulative frequency graph, the number of the men who are 185 cm and shorter than 185 cm is 40.

The number of the men, who are taller than 185 cm, is:

$50 - 40 = 10$

Answer   10   (3 marks)

15   In a regular polygon, the interior angle is seventeen times exterior angle, $x°$

15(a) Find the exterior angle

The number of sides of the regular polygon is n.

$x° = \dfrac{360°}{n}$ (1)

$17x° = \dfrac{(n-2) \times 180°}{n}$ (2)

Eq. (2) ÷ Eq. (1) $17 = \dfrac{(n-2) \times 180°}{360°} \Rightarrow n = 36 , \; x° = 10°$

Answer   10°   (4 marks)

15(b) Find the interior angle

$17x° = 170°$

Answer   170°   (3 marks)

10

16   A, B, C and D are on the circumference of a circle, DT is a tangent to the circle at
      D.

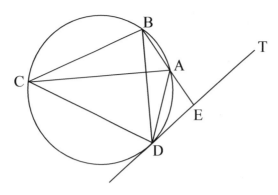

      Prove that triangle ADE is similar to triangle DBE.

      DT is a tangent to the circle at D $\Rightarrow$ $\angle$ADE = $\angle$DBE

      $\angle$AED = $\angle$BED

      $\therefore$ Triangle ADE is similar to triangle DBE (AA)

                                                            (4 marks)

17   The diagram shows a cylinder and a sphere. The base of the cylinder and the sphere
      have the same radius r cm . The ratio of their volumes, the cylinder: the sphere is 3:2.

      Work out the value of h in terms of r.

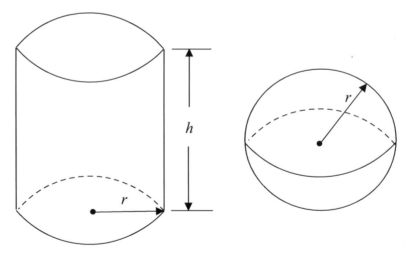

      The volume of the sphere is $\frac{4}{3}\pi r^3$

      The volume of the cylinder is $\pi r^2 h$

      $\pi r^2 h : \frac{4}{3}\pi r^3 = 3:2 \Rightarrow h = 2r$

              Answer $h = 2r$ (5 marks)

18   The diagram shows a circle, centre C. TP is a tangent to the circle and intersects the circle at P.

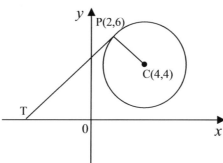

Work out the equation of line TP.

TP is a tangent to the circle, $\therefore$ TP is perpendicular to CP

The gradient of CP is $\dfrac{6-4}{2-4} = -1$, the gradient of TP is 1.

The equation of line TP passing through (2,6) with gradient 1 is:

$y - 6 = x - 2 \Rightarrow y = x + 4$

Answer $y = x + 4$ (4 marks)

19(a) Complete the table of values for $y = 6 + 2x - x^2$ and use it to draw the graph of

$y = 6 + 2x - x^2$ for values of x from -3 to 4.

When $x = -3$, $y = 6 + 2(-3) - (-3)^2 = -9$

When $x = 1$ $y = 6 + 2(1) - (1)^2 = 7$

As shown in the table and on graph.   (2 marks)

x	-3	-2	-1	0	1	2	3	4
y	**-9**	-2	3	6	7	6	3	-2

6

19(b) On the same axes, draw the graph of the line $y = x + 3$

As shown on the graph.   (2 marks)

19(c) Write down, correct to 1 decimal place, the coordinates of the point with a positive *x*-coordinate where the line meets the curve.

Answer   (2.3, 5.3)   (3 marks)

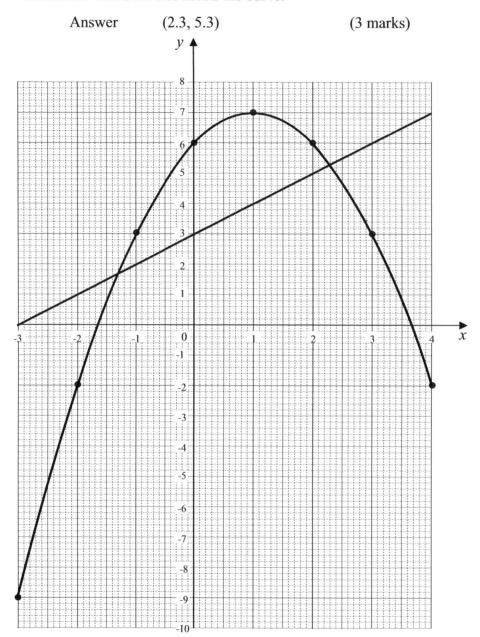

20   The sketch shows $y = \sin x$ for $0° \leq x \leq 360°$

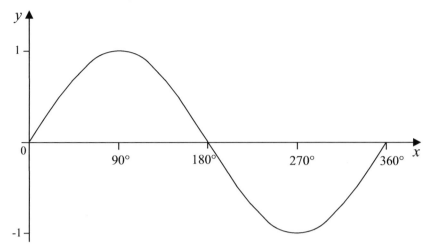

The value of $\sin 25° = 0.423$ to 3 significant figures.

20(a) Use the sketch to find another angle between $0°$ and $360°$ for which $\sin x = 0.423$.

$x = 180° - 25° = 155°$

        Answer   155°   (4 marks)

20(b) Use the sketch to find out the value of $\sin 205°$.

$\sin 205° = \sin(180° + 25°) = -\sin 25° = -0.423$

        Answer   −0.423   (4 marks)

Paper 3 solutions

1(a) Work out $2\frac{1}{6} - 1\frac{3}{4}$

$$2\frac{1}{6} - 1\frac{3}{4} = 2\frac{2}{12} - 1\frac{9}{12} = 1\frac{14}{12} - 1\frac{9}{12} = \frac{5}{12}$$

Answer $\dfrac{5}{12}$ (3 marks)

1(b) Work out $1\frac{3}{5} \div \frac{4}{7}$

Give your answer as a mixed number in its simplest form.

$$1\frac{3}{5} \div \frac{4}{7} = \frac{\overset{2}{\cancel{8}}}{5} \times \frac{7}{\underset{1}{\cancel{4}}} = \frac{14}{5} = 2\frac{4}{5}$$

Answer $2\dfrac{4}{5}$ (3 marks)

2 Simplify $\dfrac{\sin 60° + \tan 30°}{\sin 45°}$

Give your answer in the form $\dfrac{a}{b}\sqrt{c}$, where a, b and c are integers

$$\frac{\sin 60° + \tan 30°}{\sin 45°} = \frac{\frac{\sqrt{3}}{2} + \frac{\sqrt{3}}{3}}{\frac{\sqrt{2}}{2}} = \frac{(\frac{\sqrt{3}}{2} + \frac{\sqrt{3}}{3}) \times \sqrt{2}}{\frac{\sqrt{2}}{2} \times \sqrt{2}} = \frac{\frac{5\sqrt{3}}{6} \times \sqrt{2}}{\frac{2}{2}} = \frac{5}{6}\sqrt{6}$$

Answer $\dfrac{5}{6}\sqrt{6}$ (3 marks)

3 n is an integer.

Prove $(n+4)^2 - (n+2)^2$ is divisible by 4.

$$(n+4)^2 - (n+2)^2 = (n+4-n-2)(n+4+n+2) = 2(2n+6) = 4(n+3)$$

$\therefore (n+4)^2 - (n+2)^2$ is divisible by 4 (3 marks)

$\boxed{\dfrac{}{12}}$

4   Jack's solution to the inequality $-x^2 - 2x + 15 > 0$ is shown on the number line.

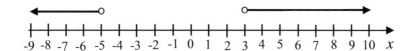

Is Jack's solution correct? Explain your reasoning.

$-x^2 - 2x + 15 > 0 \Rightarrow -(x^2 + 2x - 15) > 0 \Rightarrow (x-3)(x+5) < 0 \Rightarrow -5 < x < 3$

No, Jack's solution is shown $x < -5$, $x > 3$

The correct solution should be $-5 < x < 3$, as shown below.

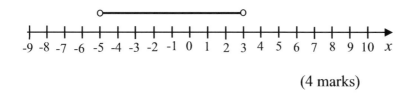

(4 marks)

5   Chocolate bars are sold in two sizes. A standard bar costs 29p and weighs 50 g. A king-size bar costs 45p and weighs 75 g.

Which size of bar is the better value for money?

The standard bar: 0.58p per gram, as $\dfrac{29}{50} = 0.58$

The king-size bar: 0.6p per gram, as $\dfrac{45}{75} = 0.6$

    Answer   Standard bar   (4 marks)

6   y is inversely proportional to x.

Complete the table.

$y = \dfrac{k}{x} \Rightarrow k = xy \Rightarrow k = 2 \times 6 = 12$

$y = \dfrac{12}{x} \Rightarrow y_1 = \dfrac{12}{3} = 4$

$x = \dfrac{k}{y} \Rightarrow x_2 = \dfrac{12}{24} = \dfrac{1}{2}$ as shown in the table.

x	3	2	$\dfrac{1}{2}$
y	4	6	24

(2 marks)

10

73

7   Rearrange $6 = \sqrt{\dfrac{wx}{x+w}}$ to make x the subject.

$$6 = \sqrt{\dfrac{wx}{x+w}} \Rightarrow 36(x+w) = wx \Rightarrow wx - 36x = 36w \Rightarrow x = \dfrac{36w}{w-36}$$

Answer $x = \dfrac{36w}{w-36}$ (3 marks)

8   a, b, c and d are four integers.

Their mean is 50, their modal is 51, and their range is 10.

8(a)   Find the value of the largest of the four integers.

$$\dfrac{x + x - 10 + 51 \times 2}{4} = 50 \Rightarrow x = 54$$

Answer   54   (4 marks)

8(b)   Find the mean value of the numbers $(2a-4)$, $(2b-4)$, $(2c-4)$ and $(2d-4)$.

The mean value of the numbers is:

$$\dfrac{2a - 4 + 2b - 4 + 2c - 4 + 2d - 4}{4} = \dfrac{2(a+b+c+d)}{4} - 4 = 2 \times 50 - 4 = 96$$

Answer   96   (4 marks)

9(a)   Write $\dfrac{1}{9}$ as a recurring decimal

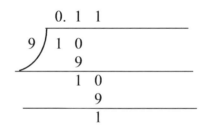

Answer $0.\dot{1}$ (3 marks)

9(b)   Write $3.0\dot{9}$ as a mixed number in its simplest form.

$x = 3.0\dot{9}$ (1)

$100x = 309.0\dot{9}$ (2)

Eq. (2) - Eq. (1) $99x = 306 \Rightarrow x = 3\dfrac{1}{11}$

Answer $3\dfrac{1}{11}$ (4 marks)

18

10(a)   Solve $x^3 = x(2x+3)$

$x^3 = x(2x+3) \Rightarrow x(x^2 - 2x - 3) = 0 \Rightarrow x(x-3)(x+1) \Rightarrow x = 0, 3 \text{ or } -1$

Answer   -1, 0, 3   (3 marks)

10(b)   Solve $\sqrt{12} + \sqrt{48} = \sqrt{27} + \sqrt{x}$

$\sqrt{12} + \sqrt{48} = \sqrt{27} + \sqrt{x} \Rightarrow 2\sqrt{3} + 4\sqrt{3} = 3\sqrt{3} + \sqrt{x} \Rightarrow \sqrt{x} = 3\sqrt{3} \Rightarrow x = 27$

Answer   27   (3 marks)

11      $f(x) = 16 - x^2 - 2x$ for all real values of x.

Solve $f(2x) = 8$

$16 - (2x)^2 - 2 \times (2x) = 8 \Rightarrow 4x^2 + 4x - 8 = 0 \Rightarrow x^2 + x - 2 = 0 \Rightarrow (x+2)(x-1) = 0$

$\Rightarrow x = -2 \text{ or } x = 1$

Answer -2 , 1   (2 marks)

12   A parabola has a equation $y = x^2 + 4x + 5$.

Prove that the parabola does not intersect the x-axis

$y = x^2 + 4x + 5 = (x+2)^2 + 1 \geq 1 \Rightarrow$ All the curve is above the x-axis.

$\therefore$ The parabola does not intersect the x-axis   (3 marks)

13   All 25 pupils in John's class took a Maths test.

John calculated that the mean mark for the class was 40.0 marks. He calculated that the median mark was 38 marks.

After John had done the calculations, Emma found that John had not given the mark in her answer to Question 4.

John awarded Emma an extra 10 marks.

13(a)   Calculate the new mean mark for the class.

$40 + \dfrac{10}{25} = 40.4$

Answer   40.4 marks   (3 marks)

14

75

Before Emma was awarded the extra marks, Emma had the fifth highest mark in the class.

13(b) What is the effect of Emma's extra marks on the median mark? Does it increase, decrease or stay the same?

Explain your answer.

Stay the same, Emma's extra marks do not affect the position of pupils placed lower than the fifth.

Answer   Stay the same   (3 marks)

14   The scatter graph shows the heights of boys at different ages.

14(a)   Draw a line of best fit on the scatter graph.   (3 marks)

A line of best fit on the scatter graph is shown below

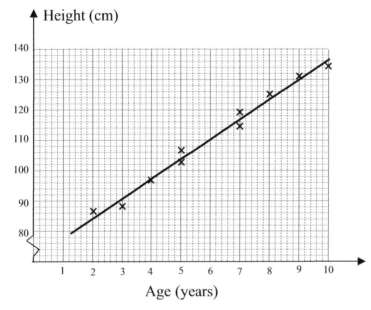

14(b)   What type of correlation is there between age and height?

It is a strong positive correlation since all the points lie roughly on a straight line going upwards from left to right.   (3 marks)

14(c)   Estimate the height of a six year old.

Answer   the height of a six year old is 110 cm

(3 marks)

15   There are 7 blue marbles and 3 red marbles in a bag. Two marbles are taken at random from the bag.

15(a) Calculate, as an exactly fraction, the probability that two marbles are different colour.

Two marbles are taken in this order, 1st blue, 2nd red. The probability is $\dfrac{7}{10} \times \dfrac{3}{9}$

Two marbles are taken in this order, 1st red, 2nd blue. The probability is $\dfrac{3}{10} \times \dfrac{7}{9}$

The probability that two marbles are different colour is $\dfrac{7}{10} \times \dfrac{3}{9} + \dfrac{3}{10} \times \dfrac{7}{9} = \dfrac{7}{15}$

Answer $\dfrac{7}{15}$ (5 marks)

15(b) Calculate, as an exactly fraction, the probability that both marbles are the same colour.

The probability, when both are red marbles, is: $\dfrac{3}{10} \times \dfrac{2}{9}$

The probability, when both are blue marbles, is: $\dfrac{7}{10} \times \dfrac{6}{9}$

$\therefore$ The probability that both marbles are the same colour is: $\dfrac{3}{10} \times \dfrac{2}{9} + \dfrac{7}{10} \times \dfrac{6}{9} = \dfrac{8}{15}$

Answer $\dfrac{8}{15}$ (5 marks)

(Alternative method: by excluding the probability that two marbles are different colour, $1 - \dfrac{7}{15} = \dfrac{8}{15}$, where $\dfrac{7}{15}$ is from part (a) above)

10

16   QPRS is a cyclic quadrilateral. PS is a diameter.

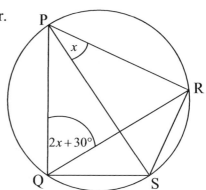

Work out the value of x.

QPRS is a cyclic quadrilateral, $\angle SQR = \angle SPR = x$ (Angles in the same segment are

equal)

PS is a diameter, $\angle SQP = 90°$ (The angle subtended at the circumference by

a semicircle is always a right angle)

$\angle SQP = \angle PQR + \angle SQR = 90° \Rightarrow 2x + 30° + x = 90° \Rightarrow x = 20°$

Answer   20°   (5 marks)

17   The square ABCD is drawn inside the regular octagon ABEFGHIJ. They share side

AB.

Work out the value of x.

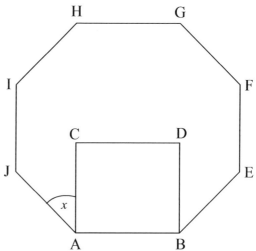

$\angle CAB = 90°$, $\angle JAB = \dfrac{(8-2)}{8} \times 180° = 135°$

$x = \angle JAB - \angle CAB = 135° - 90° = 45°$

Answer   45°   (5 marks)

18   This shape consists of a sector of a circle with 2 identical right-angled triangles.

Calculate the area of this shape.

Give your answer in terms of π.

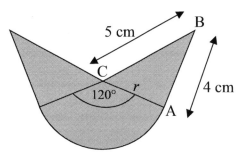

In right-angled triangle ABC, $r = \sqrt{BC^2 - AB^2} = \sqrt{5^2 - 4^2} = 3$

The area of this shape can be calculated as follows.

$$\frac{AC \times AB}{2} \times 2 + \frac{120°}{360°} \times \pi \times r^2 = \frac{3 \times 4}{2} \times 2 + \frac{120°}{360°} \times \pi \times 3^2 = 12 + 3\pi$$

Answer $(12 + 3\pi)$ cm^2 (5 marks)

19   The graph of $y = a\cos(x + b°)$, $0° \leq x < 360°$, $a > 0$, $-180 < b < 180$, is shown below.

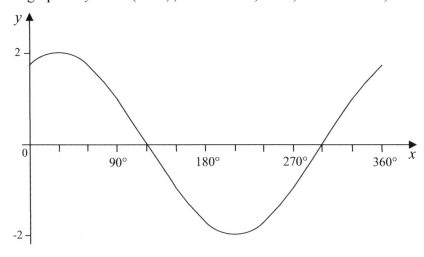

State the values of a and b.

$y = 2\cos(x - 30°)$

$a = 2$, $b = -30$

Answer $a = 2$, $b = -30$ (4 marks)

9

20   The sketch shows part of a circle, and a line $y = -2x + 6$. The line passes the centre of the circle. The circle intersects the y-axis at points A and B.

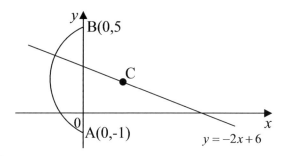

Work out the equation of the circle.

$C(C_x, C_y)$ is the centre of the circle. The circle intersects the y-axis at points A and B. $C_y = \dfrac{A_y + B_y}{2} = \dfrac{5-1}{2} = 2$

The line passes the centre of the circle, $\therefore C_y = -2C_x + 6 \Rightarrow C_x = \dfrac{6-C_y}{2} = \dfrac{6-2}{2} = 2$

The radius of the circle is $AC = \sqrt{(C_y - A_y)^2 + (C_x - A_x)^2} = \sqrt{(2+1)^2 + (2-0)^2} = \sqrt{13}$

The equation of the circle is $(x-2)^2 + (y-2)^2 = 13$

        Answer $(x-2)^2 + (y-2)^2 = 13$ (5 marks)

5

Paper 4 solutions

1   Work out

1(a) $\begin{pmatrix} 2 \\ 5 \end{pmatrix} + 3\begin{pmatrix} 5 \\ 3 \end{pmatrix}$

$$\begin{pmatrix} 2 \\ 5 \end{pmatrix} + 3\begin{pmatrix} 5 \\ 3 \end{pmatrix} = \begin{pmatrix} 2 + 3 \times 5 \\ 5 + 3 \times 3 \end{pmatrix} = \begin{pmatrix} 17 \\ 14 \end{pmatrix}$$

   Answer $\begin{pmatrix} 17 \\ 14 \end{pmatrix}$ (3 marks)

1(b) $2\begin{pmatrix} 4 \\ 3 \end{pmatrix} - 4\begin{pmatrix} 3 \\ 5 \end{pmatrix}$

$$2\begin{pmatrix} 4 \\ 3 \end{pmatrix} - 4\begin{pmatrix} 3 \\ 5 \end{pmatrix} = \begin{pmatrix} 2 \times 4 - 4 \times 3 \\ 2 \times 3 - 4 \times 5 \end{pmatrix} = \begin{pmatrix} -4 \\ -14 \end{pmatrix}$$

   Answer $\begin{pmatrix} -4 \\ -14 \end{pmatrix}$ (3 marks)

2   Express $\sqrt{40} + 4\sqrt{10} + \sqrt{90}$ as a surd in its simplest form.

$$\sqrt{40} + 4\sqrt{10} + \sqrt{90} = 2\sqrt{10} + 4\sqrt{10} + 3\sqrt{10} = 9\sqrt{10}$$

   Answer $9\sqrt{10}$ (3 marks)

3(a)   John drives 214 miles in 4 hours 53 minutes.

   Do a calculation to find an approximate value for his average speed.

$$\frac{214 \text{ miles}}{4 \text{ hr } 53 \text{ min}} \approx \frac{200 \text{ miles}}{5 \text{ hr}} = 40 \text{ mph}$$

   Answer   40 mph   (3 marks)

3(b)   Is your approximate value greater or less than John's actual average speed?

   Explain your answer.

   Answer   Less, as rounding 214 miles down and 4 hours 53 minutes up,

   both make the approximation smaller than the actual number.

   (3 marks)

15

4 In a tennis club, $\frac{3}{5}$ of the members are women, $\frac{1}{4}$ of the members are men, and the rest of the members are children.

4(a) What percentage of the members are children?

$$1-(\frac{3}{5}+\frac{1}{4})=1-\frac{17}{20}=\frac{3}{20}=0.15=15\%$$

Answer   15%   (3 marks)

4(b) Find the ration women : children

$$\frac{3}{5}:\frac{3}{20}=4:1$$

Answer   4:1   (3 marks)

4(c) There are 15 children in the club, find the total number of members in the club.

The ratio women : children $= 4:1$

The number of women is 60, as $15\times 4=60$

The ratio men : women $=\frac{1}{4}:\frac{3}{5}=5:12$

The number of men is $\frac{5\times 60}{12}=25$

$25+60+15=100$

Answer   100   (3 marks)

5(a) Fully factorise $(x^2-9)-(x-3)(3x+5)$

$(x^2-9)-(x-3)(3x+5)=(x-3)(x+3-3x-5)=-2(x-3)(x+1)$.

Answer $-2(x-3)(x+1)$ (3 marks)

5(b) By factorising fully, simplify $\dfrac{x^4-4x^3+3x^2}{x^4-10x^2+9}$

$$\frac{x^4-4x^3+3x^2}{x^4-10x^2+9}=\frac{x^2(x^2-4x+3)}{(x^2-1)(x^2-9)}=\frac{x^2(x-1)(x-3)}{(x-1)(x+1)(x-3)(x+3)}=\frac{x^2}{(x+1)(x+3)}$$

Answer $\dfrac{x^2}{(x+1)(x+3)}$ (3 marks)

15

6 A bus has some passengers on board at starting station. At the first stop two fifths get off and then 7 people get on. At the next stop a quarter of the people remaining on the bus get off and then 13 get on. There are 34 passengers on board now.

How many passengers are there on the bus at starting station?

The number of passengers at starting station is x

At the first stop, the number of passengers is: $x - \dfrac{2}{5}x + 7 = \dfrac{3}{5}x + 7$

At the next stop, the number of passengers is: $\dfrac{3}{5}x + 7 - \dfrac{1}{4}(\dfrac{3}{5}x + 7) + 13 = \dfrac{9}{20}x + 20 - \dfrac{7}{4}$

$\dfrac{9}{20}x + 20 - \dfrac{7}{4} = 34 \Rightarrow x = 35$

   Answer   35   (3 marks)

7(a) Expand and simplify $(2x + 3y)(3x - 2y)$

$(2x + 3y)(3x - 2y) = 6x^2 + 9xy - 4xy - 6y^2 = 6x^2 + 5xy - 6y^2$

   Answer $6x^2 + 5xy - 6y^2$ (3 marks)

7(b) Write as a single fraction $\dfrac{6}{x^2 - 9} - \dfrac{1}{x - 3}$

Give your answer in its simplest form.

$\dfrac{6}{x^2 - 9} - \dfrac{1}{x - 3} = \dfrac{6}{(x-3)(x+3)} - \dfrac{1}{x-3} = \dfrac{6 - x - 3}{(x-3)(x+3)} = -\dfrac{1}{x+3}$

   Answer $-\dfrac{1}{x+3}$ (3 marks)

8 a, b, c and d are consecutive integers.

Explain why $(a + b)(c + d)$ is always odd.

Let $b = a + 1$, $c = a + 2$, $d = a + 3$

$(a + b)(c + d) = (a + a + 1)(a + 2 + a + 3) = 4a^2 + 12a + 5 = 4(a^2 + 3a) + 5$

$4(a^2 + 3a)$ is always even

$\therefore$ $4(a^2 + 3a) + 5$ is always odd.

$\therefore$ $(a + b)(c + d)$ is always odd

        (4 marks)

13

9   You are given that $5.6 \times 13.2 = 73.92$ exactly.

9(a)   Emma says that $56 \times 0.0132 = 7.392$

Without doing an exact calculation, show that Emma is wrong.

$$\frac{56}{5.6} = 10 \, , \quad \frac{0.0132}{13.2} = 0.001$$

$$56 \times 0.0132 = 73.92 \times 10 \times 0.001 = 73.92 \times 0.01 = 0.7392$$

(3 marks)

9(b)   Find the exact value of 0.056×132

$$0.056 \times 132 = 0.01 \times 10 \times 73.92 = 7.392$$

Answer   7.392   (3 marks)

10    $x : y = 3 : 4$ and z is 20% of y.

Work out $x : y : z$

Give your answer in its simplest form.

$$x : y = 3 : 4 \Rightarrow x : y = 15 : 20 \qquad (1)$$

$$z = 20\% y \Rightarrow y : z = 100 : 20 \Rightarrow y : z = 20 : 4 \qquad (2)$$

$$x : y : z = 15 : 20 : 4$$

Answer $15 : 20 : 4$ (3 marks)

11   The four candidates in an election were A, B, C and D.

The pie chart shows the proportion of votes for each candidate.

Work out the probability that a person who voted, chosen at random, voted for A.

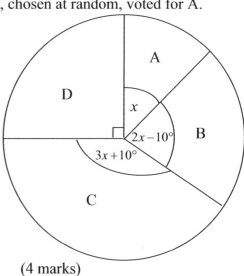

$$x + (2x - 10°) + (3x + 10°) + 90° = 360° \Rightarrow x = \frac{270°}{6} = 45°$$

The probability that a person voted for A is

$$\frac{45°}{360°} = \frac{1}{8}$$

Answer $\frac{1}{8}$ (4 marks)

13

12 There are

8 different sandwiches

5 different drinks

and

3 different snacks.

Meal Deal
Choose one sandwich, one drink and one snack

12(a) How many different Meal Deal combinations are there?

$8 \times 5 \times 3 = 120$

Answer 120 (3 marks)

12(b) Two of the sandwiches have cheese in them.

Three of the drinks are fizzy.

Emma picks a Meal Deal at random.

Work out the probability that the sandwich has cheese in it and the drink is fizzy.

Give your answer as a fraction in its simplest form.

Meal Deal combinations for the cheese sandwich and fizzy drink are:

$2 \times 3 \times 3 = 18$

The probability, that the sandwich has cheese in it and the drink is fizzy, is:

$\frac{18}{120} = \frac{3}{20}$

Answer $\frac{3}{20}$ (3 marks)

(Alternative method: the probability, that the sandwich has cheese in it, is $\frac{2}{8}$; the probability, that the drink is fizzy, is $\frac{3}{5}$; the probability, that the sandwich has cheese in it and the drink is fizzy, is: $\frac{2}{8} \times \frac{3}{5} = \frac{3}{20}$)

6

13   Emma is a member of a video club.

She pays a fixed charge of £20 every six months.

She pays an additional charge for every video she hires.

The line on the graph shows cost for six months to Emma for up to 20 videos hired.

13(a) Calculate the cost of hiring each of the first 20 videos.

The line is passing through points (0, 20) and (20, 35)

The gradient of the line is $\dfrac{35-20}{20-0} = 0.75$

Therefore the cost of hiring each of the first 20 videos is 75p.

Answer   75p   (3 marks)

Once she has hired 20 videos in any six month period, she pays only 50p for every additional video she hires.

13(b) Draw a line on the graph so that the graph can be used to calculate the total cost in a six-month period of hiring up to 50 videos.

The total cost in a six-month period of hiring up to 50 videos is

$y = 35 + 0.5(x - 20) \Rightarrow y = 25 + 0.5x$, where $20 < x \le 50$

Line $y = 25 + 0.5x$, where $20 < x \le 50$, is drawn on the graph as shown below.

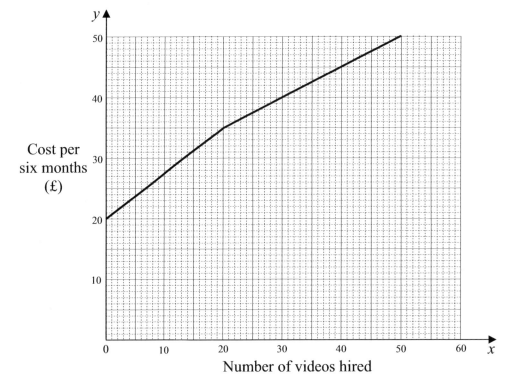

Cost per six months (£)

Number of videos hired

(3 marks)

6

14   Two congruent regular polygons are joined together.

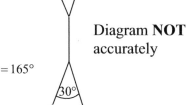

Diagram **NOT**
accurately

Work out the number of sides on each polygon.

The interior angle of the regular polygons is $\dfrac{360° - 30°}{2} = 165°$

$\dfrac{n-2}{n} \times 180° = 165° \Rightarrow n = 24$

        Answer   24   (3 marks)

15   In the diagram shown below:

ABE is a tangent to the circle with centre O

$\angle DBE = 58°$

Calculate $\angle CAB$.

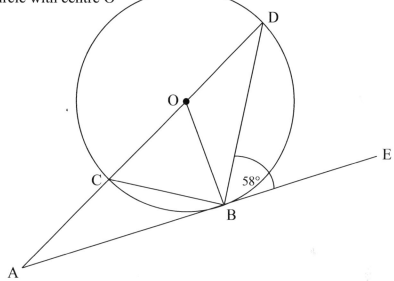

ABE is a tangent to the circle , $\angle DBE = 58° \Rightarrow \angle OCB = 58°$ (The angle between the

tangent ABE and chord BD is equal to the angle in the other segment)

OC = OB (they are radiuses of the circle). $\angle OBC = \angle OCB = 58°$

In isosceles triangle OBC, $\angle COB = 180° - \angle OCB - \angle OBC = 180° - 58° \times 2 = 64°$

$\angle OBA = 90°$ (OB is perpendicular to ABE)

In right-angled triangle ABO

$\angle CAB = 90° - \angle COB = 90° - 64° = 26°$

        Answer   26°   (3 marks)

16   A rectangle has a length of x cm and a width of y cm.

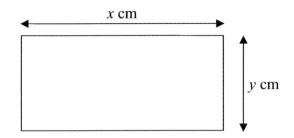

The rectangle has a perimeter of 13 cm and an area of 10 cm^2.

16(a) Show that $2x^2 - 13x + 20 = 0$

The rectangle has a perimeter of 13 cm $2x + 2y = 13$ (1)

The rectangle has an area of 10 cm^2 $xy = 10$ (2)

From Eq. (1), $y = \dfrac{13 - 2x}{2}$ (3)

From Eqs. (2) and (3), $x \times \dfrac{13 - 2x}{2} = 10 \Rightarrow 13x - 2x^2 = 20 \Rightarrow 2x^2 - 13x + 20 = 0$

(3 marks)

16(b) Solve the equation $2x^2 - 13x + 20 = 0$

$2x^2 - 13x + 20 = 0 \Rightarrow (x-4)(2x-5) = 0 \Rightarrow x = 4 \text{ or } x = 2\dfrac{1}{2}$

Answer $4 , 2\dfrac{1}{2}$ (2 marks)

5

88

17   The vectors **p** and **q** are shown in the diagram below.

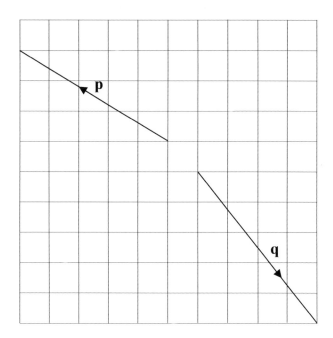

17(a) Draw **v** = **p** + **q**.

As shown on the graph **v** = $\overrightarrow{BC}$ (3 marks)

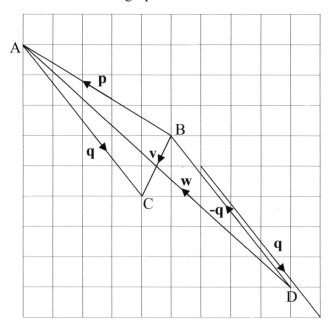

17(b) Draw **w** = **p** - **q**.

As shown on the graph **w** = $\overrightarrow{DA}$ (3 marks)

6

18   The line L_1 in the diagram has a gradient of 3, and it passes through the point (0, 2).

The line L_2 is perpendicular to L_1 and also passes through the point (0, 2).

Find the equation of the line L_2.

Give your answer in the form $y = mx + b$

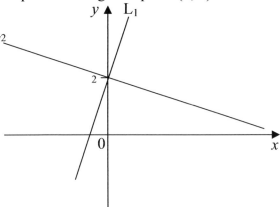

The line L_1 in the diagram has a gradient of 3, and the line L_2 is perpendicular to L_1.

Thus the gradient of L_2 is $-\dfrac{1}{3}$

The line L_2 passes through the point (0, 2), the equation of L_2 is:

$$y - 2 = -\frac{1}{3}x \Rightarrow y = -\frac{1}{3}x + 2$$

Answer $y = -\dfrac{1}{3}x + 2$ (3 marks)

19   David invests money into an account which pays a fixed rate of compound interest each year. The value, £P, of his investment after t years is given by the formula

$$P = 15000 \times 1.05^t$$

19(a) How much money did David invest?

Answer   £15000   (2 marks)

19(b) What rate of compound interest is paid each year?

Answer   5%   (2 marks)

19(c) Which graph is the best to represent the growth in David's account?

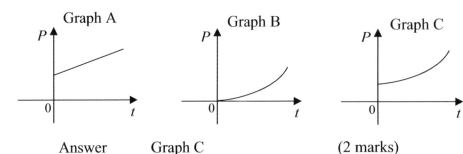

Answer   Graph C   (2 marks)

20   A flea jumps from point A and lands at point B. Its path is that of a parabola with

equation $y = \dfrac{-x^2 + 6x + 16}{2}$, where x is the horizontal distance travelled and y is its

height. All measurements are in centimetres.

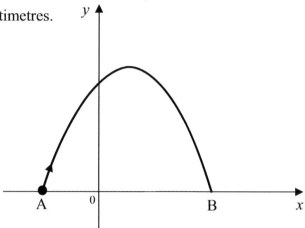

20(a) Calculate how far the flea has travelled horizontally from A to B.

$y = \dfrac{-x^2 + 6x + 16}{2}$, $\dfrac{-x^2 + 6x + 16}{2} = 0 \Rightarrow x^2 - 6x - 16 = 0 \Rightarrow (x+2)(x-8) = 0 \Rightarrow$

$A_x = -2$, $B_x = 8$, $AB = B_x - A_x = 8 + 2 = 10$

Answer   10 cm   (3 marks)

20(b) Calculate the maximum height reached by the flea during its jump.

$y = \dfrac{-x^2 + 6x + 16}{2} = \dfrac{-(x-3)^2 + 25}{2} \Rightarrow y \leq \dfrac{25}{2} \Rightarrow y \leq 12.5$

Answer   12.5 cm   (3 marks)

6

Printed in Great Britain
by Amazon